'dd

Ancient Routes and ... Roads

Photographs and Text
Jean Napier MA arps

Gwasg Carreg Gwalch

First published in 2017
© Jean Napier MA arps / Gwasg Carreg Gwalch

Published by Gwasg Carreg Gwalch,
12 Iard yr Orsaf, Llanrwst, Conwy, LL26 0EH.
tel: 01492 642031 Ffacs: 01492 641502
email: llyfrau@carreg-gwalch.com
website: www.carreg-gwalch.com

ISBN: 978-1-84524-271-8

Cover photos: **Jean Napier**

Previous Books

Jean Napier
Rhosydd – A Personal View/Golwg Bersonol
ISBN 978-0-86381-470-9

Jean Napier with Alun John Richards

A Tale of Two Rivers	ISBN 978-0-86381-989-1
Two Snowdonia Rivers	ISBN 978-0-84527-206-7
The River Conwy	ISBN 978-1-84527-288-3

All Published by Gwasg Carreg Gwalch, Llanrwst

In Memory of Cati
My Best Ever Photography
Assistant and Friend

This book is dedicated to
all who take care of
the Welsh Landscape

Contents

Introduction

I have been exploring the county of Meirionnydd for many years and find the varied landscape endlessly fascinating and one particular area, the Rhinogydd Mountains and surrounding high moorland, is especially captivating.

This land abounds with the remains of human habitation dating back through the centuries; ancient tombs, hillforts and stone circles, to name but a few. Also the old workings and waste tips from hundreds of derelict lead, gold, manganese mines and slate quarries litter the land revealing the extensive industrial activity that once existed here.

I have spent many delightful hours following the ancient trackways through this land once travelled by man and beast on their way to market and their places of work. The local farmers believe that there are fewer people living and working in this wild upland area now than at any time in human history and there are precious few locations that this can be said about today.

Many mountain farms are now deserted and the drovers' inns and overnight stopping places just ruins. Although the upside to this is that nature has been given the opportunity to reclaim her land and offer wildlife a place of refuge.

In this small book I have endeavoured to convey my passion for this unique area and give you just a small taste of what can be discovered here.

Jean Napier

above: Jean's photograph by Ken Bridges;
opposite: Bronze Age track

Foreword

The Rhinogydd, that rough and heathery mountainous spine running north-south between Dyffryn Maentwrog and Dyffryn Mawddach in the north-western quarter of the old county of Meirionnydd, has a character all of its own which sets it very much apart from the rest of Eryri.

It is a truly ancient landscape in more than one sense. These mountains are composed of very hard and acid rocks formed during that very early geological period known as the Cambrian, over 500 million years ago. It was here in the Rhinogydd that the early 19th century geologists found and first defined the Cambrian period and many of the classic rock types from which it is formed. This

Rhinogydd: Ancient Routes and Old Roads

means that wherever Cambrian rocks are met with in other parts of the world, whether in Canada, China or elsewhere, it is the Rhinogydd that provide the definitive rock types which gives us the baseline for comparisons between these areas.

The blocky, broken rock layers so characteristic of the area are hardly found anywhere else in Eryri making it very different from the rugged volcanic landscape which surrounds it. To the north, east and south are the 450–500 million year old Ordovician rocks (named after the Ordovices – the Celtic tribe who inhabited this area in pre-Roman times) and which confront you in the dramatic scarp face of Cadair Idris to the south and Yr Wyddfa (*Snowdon*) and her rugged crew to the north.

Human occupation of the area is also long-standing and, given that so little modern ploughing has happened here, the signs of ancient settlement and agriculture are everywhere. The slopes of Ardudwy forming the western part of the Rhinogydd leading down to the coast are recognised as one of the richest areas throughout the countries of Britain in terms of the sheer numbers and diversity of archaeological remains. Grazing by sheep and cattle has caused very little damage to ancient remains, unlike a plough.

Today hardly any sheep graze the heathery northern Rhinogydd. It was always difficult to find them let alone round them up from the extremely broken terrain so sheep grazing was abandoned over much of the area and left to those horny characters, the goats.

Ancient rocks, an ancient undisturbed landscape, heather-clad and wild, centuries old and quite poetic Welsh place-names linking past with present imbue the Rhinogydd with a sense of timelessness and mystery which is a world removed from humanity's frenetic and destructive pace. This place can have a profound impact on those more spiritually inclined souls, of which Jean Napier is certainly one.

Here is: "*Lle i enaid gael llonydd*" (where a soul may find peace).

Twm Elias

Information

Historical Ages

Neolithic/
New Stone Age: 4000 – 2400 BC
Bronze Age: 2400 – 700 BC
Iron Age: 700 BC – 48 AD
Roman Era: 43 – 450 AD
Medieval Era
(approx):   500 – 1400 AD

Historical Disclaimer:

During the research for this book I have come across conflicting historical opinions and information pertaining to this part of Meirionnydd. When deciding which to include, I have taken into account conversations with local historians and farmers, coupled with my own experience and knowledge of the area.

Acknowledgements

The puplishers wish to acknowledge their gratitude for these images:

National Library of Wales *p. 52, 64, 75, 82*
Gwynedd Archives *p. 36, 41, 96, 99*
Iron Bridge Museum *p. 46*
© **Jessica Evans** Gerddi Bluog Dilys 4 *p. 118*
Historical artefacts courtesy Ceredigion Museum *p. 72, 86*

Standing stones beside ancient tracks

An Ancient Land

The upland area of the Rhinogydd is steeped in history and littered with the ancient remains of human habitation. These historical sites have managed to survive, relatively intact, due mainly to their inaccessibility because of the difficult terrain and the lack of ingress by modern roads.

I have spent many delightful hours exploring this mountainous part of Meirionnydd and have selected a few of my favourite haunts to introduce you to this unique landscape.

It is evident from the great number of ruined farms and abandoned mines in this area that the land has seen a much greater human occupation over the centuries. The upland farmers I have spoken to believe there are fewer people living and working here now than at any time in human history. The locations of the sites mentioned below are marked on the map and I have provided grid references should you wish to visit. Be aware that the land can be rough, muddy and steep in places – good footwear and appropriate clothing, plus the relevant OS map and compass, are important. Please take care, observe the Countryside Code and have respect for these ancient landmarks.

Bryn Cader Faner SH 648 353

This is the most spectacular Bronze Age stone circle I have visited in Wales for both its magnificence and stunning location. Bryn Cader Faner can be seen from afar due to its prominent position at the junction of two ancient roads at the northern end of the Rhinogydd ridge. One of these roads runs from Llanfair on the coast over to Trawsfynydd and dates from the Bronze Age. Standing stones and hut circles line this trackway including the spectacular prehistoric Moel Goedog hillfort.

Frances Lynch writes in her book about Bryn Cader Faner in *A Guide to Ancient and Historic Wales*, '*it is a small cairn measuring 8 metres across, about 1metre high and round the edge are a ring of tall slabs set at an angle looking like a crown and was originally thought to have been twice the size*'. She also claims '*it was the burial site of an important person and has a cist/grave in the centre*'.

Before the Second World War the British Army removed some of the stones

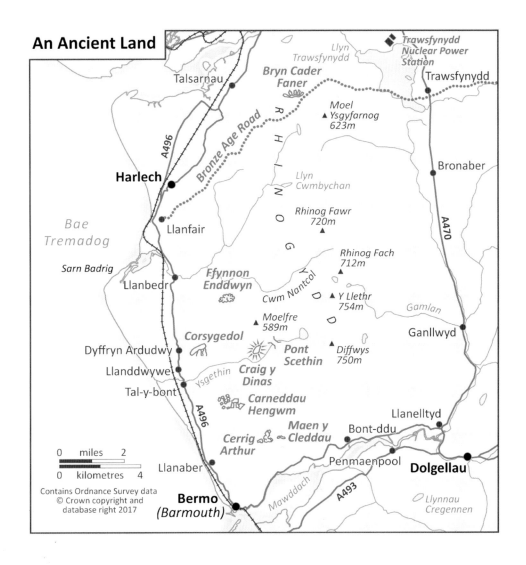

An Ancient Land

Talsarnau

Bryn Cader Faner

Llyn Trawsfynydd

Trawsfynydd Nuclear Power Station

Trawsfynydd

Bronze Age Road

Moel Ysgyfarnog 623m

Harlech

Bae Tremadog

Llanfair

Llyn Cwmbychan

Rhinog Fawr 720m

Bronaber

Sarn Badrig

Llanbedr

Ffynnon Enddwyn

Rhinog Fach 712m

Cwm Nantcol

Y Llethr 754m

Gamlan

Moelfre 589m

Dyffryn Ardudwy

Corsygedol

Pont Scethin

Diffwys 750m

Ganllwyd

Llanddwywe

Ysgethin

Craig y Dinas

Tal-y-bont

Carneddau Hengwm

Llanelltyd

Maen y Cleddau

Bont-ddu

Cerrig Arthur

Penmaenpool

Dolgellau

Llanaber

Bermo (Barmouth)

Mawddach

Llynnau Cregennen

0 miles 2

0 kilometres 4

Contains Ordnance Survey data © Crown copyright and database right 2017

on the east side and those remaining were used as target practice, the army showing a total disregard for this precious site! Luckily, it has survived this modern-day sacrilege more or less intact but only 18 of the tall stones that form the outer circle remain instead of the original count which was thought to be nearer 30.

In the 1920s, a local farmer frequently visited the stone circle to investigate the grave but each time he attempted to dig, thunder and lightening crashed down around him and he fled in terror – coincidence? His great-grandson told me this story.

People often say that these ancient sites bestow a strange sense of timelessness when in their vicinity which can only partly be put down to their isolated position and the lack of nearby modern-day reference points. This curious atmosphere is especially prevalent around Bryn Cader Faner and I have often felt an overwhelming sense of time seeming to stand still when I have lingered within the stone circle.

Cerrig Arthur SH 631 188

This is one of several sites in northwest Wales named after the mythical hero King Arthur. The remains of this Bronze Age stone circle, thought to be a ritual or burial monument, are located two miles north-east on a narrow lane high above Barmouth on a junction of old tracks and the surrounding area is called Cae'r Cerrig. The two tallest stones are possibly the entrance but stumps of others are just visible marking an oval of about 14m across.

Julian Heath writes in Sacred Circles – '*John Hoyle, historian, feels that the longest axis of the oval was deliberately orientated on the distant escarpment of Craig-y-Llyn on Cader where, in 1700BC, the moon would have risen from its most southerly position. Also a burial cairn on Craig-y-Llyn can be seen and perhaps there is some connection between the two monuments*'.

From here, the majestic Cader Idris dominates the scene with the beautiful Mawddach river flowing through the valley below. As with many of the stone circles in Wales, it is possible that they were deliberately positioned high up in the landscape in order to allow wide-ranging views from these 'sacred' sites.

According to David Berry in *The*

previous page: Bryn Cader Faner; opposite: Cerrig Arthur

Rhinogydd: Ancient Routes and Old Roads

Rhinogydd: Ancient Routes and Old Roads

Mawddach-Ardudwy Trail, the site is very close to the original placement meant for a local church and is known as 'church stones'. Legend claims that the church's foundations were repeatedly demolished overnight by an unseen power and a voice was heard calling loudly "Llanaber, Llanaber". This terrified the builders so much that they changed the location of the church to the village of Llanaber near the coast!

Ffynnon Enddwyn SH 614 254

Known as a Holy Well or Sacred Spring, tradition says that Saint Enddwyn (patron saint of Llanenddwyn) was cured from a 'sore disease' after bathing in this well. An information board at the site says:

> "One day, journeying to Trawsfynydd, she bathed and refreshed herself in the well and was cured. Sick folk from all parts resorted to it to be cured from gland-related illnesses, skin diseases, sore eyes and arthritis. It was a tradition to drink the water and apply some of the moss that grew beside the wall as a plaster. People left their crutches and sticks behind as tokens of their restoration, and others threw pins into the well to ward off evil spirits."

In the 18th century, a wooden roof was added to create a bathing chamber although this has long since perished. The well is marked on the OS map as simply '*spring*' and the church of Saint Endwyn in the village of Llaneddwyn are both named after the saint but, unfortunately, very little is known about Saint Enddwyn and even the gender of the Saint is disputed.

I have often drunk the sweet-tasting well water and all I can say is that, at the present time, I have no arthritis or skin diseases (touch wood)!

above left: Horse pen;
left & right:. Ffynnon Enddwyn

Craig y Dinas *SH 624 231*

This impressive Iron Age hillfort dominates the wide Scethin valley and is built on a natural rocky promontory. It blends so well into the landscape that, from a distance, it can hardly be identified. It is surrounded by swampy ground except on the north side where the fort can be accessed via a narrow causeway along a small ridge. Inside a massive bank of earth and boulders there are three lines of interconnecting stone walls, some of them 12 to 15 feet thick. COFLEIN describes Craig y Dinas as a *"Stone walled polygonal hillfort 75mx40m with outworks extending 14m to NE, and extensive entrance works (walled trackway and stone clearance) to SE".*

Due to its size and location, it is thought to have been a place of refuge for local inhabitants and their animals; remains of roundhouse settlements, low meandering field-walls and other signs of past human habitation surround the base of the hillfort.

I have often stood high up on the topmost escarpment from where there is an impressive vantage point across the valley and down towards the sea and tried to imagine the fear and panic felt by the local people fleeing to the hillfort as invaders were seen approaching all those years ago.

Craig y Dinas

Carneddau Hengwm *SH 613 205*

The National Trust have produced a leaflet which outlines a circular walk of about four miles from Egryn Abbey, near Tal-y-bont, that takes in Pen Dinas hillfort and a whole string of standing stones, hut circles and tombs up in the hills above. Carneddau Hengwm is the most spectacular of these and consists of two Neolithic burial chambers dated about 3000 BC. '*The southern-most cairn has an entrance to a tomb and was probably about 200 feet but from the great deal of destruction is not possible to give an accurate figure. It is probable that the present appearance of the southern cairn is due to the piling up of stones over the last hundred years for the purpose of clearing the ground. The northern cairn is at present 100 feet long and the destruction has been considerable and only one large capstone remains out of several that were formerly present*' – Information: Gwynedd Archaeological Trust.

Hundreds of tons of stones were subsequently pillaged from the original tombs to build the early 19th century enclosure walls that now dissect the site. The builders helped themselves to the

Carneddau Hengwm

loose stones and this possibly accounts for the extensive damage including the broken capstones and their supports. The ruined portal dolmen at the east end still has two impressive standing stones but the large capstone is now lying free alongside.

It is known from a description in *Tours in Wales* written by Thomas Pennant, the Welsh naturalist, antiquarian and writer, that these walls did not exist at the time of his visit in 1780. He also comments on one of the tombs – "*It is now converted into a retreat for a shepherd who has placed stone seats within and there was a fireplace built into a wall with a chimney formed of loose stones placed above.*"

Huw Dylan Owen mentions in *Meini Meirionnydd* that Madog ap Llewellyn in the 13th and Owain Glyndŵr in the 14th century were both known to have passed Hengwm with their armies on their way to attack Harlech.

Tourists were able to visit the site in the 18th and 19th centuries because, at that time, it was close to one of the main thoroughfares that ran from the coast of Ardudwy, via Bwlch y Rhiwgyr to Dolgellau.

Corsygedol (Arthur's Quoit)

SH 603 228

The remains of the burial chamber known as Corsygedol lie ¼ mile south east of the historic mansion of the Vaughan's of the same name. '*This Neolithic burial chamber now only consists of three stones: two uprights supporting a large capstone but there are a large number of stones strewn around the area which must have belonged to the original cairn. The structural remains stand within the eastern end of a long, low mound of earth and stones roughly 84 feet long and 44 feet wide at its maximum point.*' Information: Gwynedd Archaeological Trust.

The wide valley of the Yscethin river is strewn with the evidence of early civilisation and Frances Lynch writes in *A Guide to Ancient and Historic Wales* – '*it forms part of an exceptionally extensive and well-preserved ancient landscape containing settlement sites and field systems dating from late prehistoric and Roman times through to the medieval period*'. As with many of these sites, stones were removed from the tomb to build the nearby walls. Drawings by William Stukley, who visited the site with Thomas Pennant in the late 1700s, show that the damage was done to the tomb

Corsygedol burial chamber

before this time. Despite this desecration it is, in my opinion, a beautiful tomb to visit. There is a small car parking area situated on a narrow road 400 metres past the Corsygedol estate (fee £1 in a box). It is only a short distance to the site along a tarmac track and one of the few ancient places that could be accessed by wheelchair.

Pont Scethin *SH 635 234*

One of my favourite north-south walks through the Rhinogydd takes in this magnificent 12th century bridge over the Scethin river on my journey between Dolgellau and Tal-y-bont on the coast. Situated in splendid isolation, it forms part of a once strategic route linking Bont-ddu on the Mawddach and Harlech. Marker stones placed along the route across the moor indicate it was an ancient trackway long before it became an important medieval route used as a packhorse trail and possibly a coaching road (this subject is covered in depth in The Old London-to-Harlech Road chapter).

above: Corsygedol
opposite & next page: Pont Scethin

The bridge sits in middle of the wide and boggy Ysgethin valley and was the only crossing point until the 1770s when William Vaughan of Corsygedol had Pont Fadog built over the Yscethin at a point closer to the sea. (The bridge's significance for the drovers is explored in a later chapter.)

Many legends and stories about the fairies and their magic are told about the remote Yscethin valley and it is said that the Druids worshiped here and used the stones near Pont Scethin as an altar. The people of Ardudwy believed that Llyn Irddyn, tucked under Llawllech ridge near Pont Scethin, was sacred and that the water had healing powers – Information: *Meini Meirionnydd.*

This is an extremely isolated lake and would have required a great deal of faith in its curative powers to undertake such an arduous journey.

This is tough mountain bike land and routes in this area feature in many of the magazines for this sport. Unfortunately 4x4s and off-road bikes are legally allowed to use it and this has led to a substantial amount of damage being done to this fragile track.

Cerrig y Cledd / Maen y Cleddau *SH 642 197*

Cerrig y Cledd standing stone is now hidden deep in a pine forest planted in the 1950s.

It gets its name from Maen y Cleddau, a massive stone that lies on the ground in the trees near-by. This stone has been split into three by ice, and two of the stones bear natural parallel cuts made by ice movement that look rather like the imprint made by a large sword – hence the given name.

Early man is thought to have linked Maen y Cleddau with Cerrig Arthur stone circle situated high up on the skyline above.

Cerrig Arthur would have been visible before the forest was planted that now obscures this view today.

The connection between these two stones supposedly reinforced the legend surrounding King Arthur's sword being pulled from a stone – Information: *Meini Meirionnydd*.

opposite: Cerrig y Cledd;
above: Maen y Cleddau

A Modern 'Relic'? *SH 691 381*

The massive twin towers of Trawsfynydd Nuclear Power Station are visible from the whole of the east side of the Rhinogydd. I know it is not ancient but I can't resist its inclusion here, as its impact on the landscape will probably outlast any of the other ancient sites previously mentioned.

'*It started service in 1965 and ceased electricity generation in 1991 but the continuing decommissioning process will take many more years to complete. It is thought that the height of the main buildings will be reduced by 2026 and final site clearance is not projected to start until 2076 with the land returned to its original state by 2083*'. (BBC Science 28 October 2013). There is a rumour that a possible 'new mini-nuclear power plant' could be developed here – discussion is currently underway.

W M Condry comments in his book *The Snowdonia National Park* – '*The deliberate placing of a nuclear power station in the heart of wild Wales and in the very centre of a National Park is surely a violent negation of everything a National Park stands for*'.

Like all developments, they can be a double-edged sword; whilst there is no doubt that the Power Station is still bringing work and income to a poor, economic area, I wonder whether the production of electricity for just 26 years is worth the possible risks to the environment and the ongoing enormous decommissioning costs?

Trawsfynydd Power Station

The Old London-to-Harlech Road

The focus of this chapter is the section of the London-to-Harlech road that crosses the Rhinogydd Mountains between Bontddu, near Dolgellau, and Harlech on the coast as shown on the Map.

It has been an amazing experience for me following in the footsteps of thousands of people and animals that have travelled this way over the millennia. I have often sat high up on Lawlledd, the Diffwys ridge, and looked down onto the wide sweep of the Ysgethin valley below and wondered about the day-to-day lives of the people that lived there centuries ago.

An Ancient Road

This road, thought to have been in existence for thousands of years, is still the most direct route between Harlech and Dolgellau. Craig y Dinas, the Iron Age hillfort mentioned in a previous chapter, is situated close to the road and the area around the hillfort is surrounded by standing stones and the remnants of human habitation that date back through the centuries.

The Romans may have come this way to access the coast from their main camp and marching ground further inland at Tolmen y Mur near Bronaber. However, Bwlch Tyddiad Pass, (often called the 'Roman Steps'), is an ancient way through the Rhinogydd to Trawsfynydd via Cwm Bychan, and would have been in use long before the Roman era.

The large, flat stones, however, were probably laid in medieval times to aid the transportation of goods to the coast by packhorse. It is known from 20th century excavations carried out by Peter Crew that, in the late 14th century, iron ingots from smelters at Bwlch y Ffordd and nearby sites would have been carried by packhorse over Bwlch Tyddiad to Harlech Castle – this area is now covered by Coed y Brenin conifer forest.

In 1765 William Vaughan, proprietor of Corsygedol, carried out a great deal of improvements to the old road including the laying of milestones marking the route that can still be seen today.

The Old London-to-Harlech Road

Llyn Trawsfynydd

Trawsfynydd

Talsarnau

Moel Ysgyfarnog
623m ▲

Bronaber

Castle

Harlech

A496

Llyn Cwmbychan

Llanfair

Bae Tremadog

Rhinog Fawr
720m ▲

A470

Sarn Badrig

Rhinog Fach
712m ▲

Llanbedr

R H I N O G   Y   D   D

Cwm Nantcol

Y Llethr
754m ▲

Gamlan

Moelfre
589m ▲

Corsygedol

Pont Scethin

Diffwys
750m ▲

Ganllwyd

Dyffryn Ardudwy

Janet Haigh Monument

Llanddwywe

Ysgethin

Llawllech

Marker Stone

Llanelltyd

Cymer Abbey

Tal-y-bont

A496

P

Bont-ddu

Dolgellau

Llanaber

Penmaenpool

London

→

Contains Ordnance Survey data
© Crown copyright and
database right 2017

0 miles 2
0 kilometres 4

Bermo (Barmouth)

Mawddach

A493

Llynnau Cregennen

The Route through the Rhinogydd

The start of this route can be accessed from a small parking area at the end of a narrow tarmac road that leads up from Bont-ddu. It initially ascends a steep, rocky track to where it splits into two by a massive marker stone – one side saying "*From TalyBont 1111M*" the other "*From Harlech XM*". The left-hand Tal-y-bont track was an early road over to Barmouth also used by the drovers descending Bwlch y Rhiwgyr on their way from the coast towards Dolgellau and all places east.

The right-hand Harlech track continues northward climbing up the Braich to the top of Llawllech ridge on Diffwys Mountain where the occasional glance behind can provide a fantastic view of Cader Idris and the Mawddach below. The track descends steeply in zigzags to the valley floor where it crosses over Pont Scethin, circles around the west side of Moelfre and then travels on to Harlech via Llanfair.

John Ogilby and his team undertook a very early survey of Welsh roads in 1675 from which a series of maps were produced. The one covering this area, named the *The Road from Welshpool to Carnarvan* (*Atlas Meirionnydd*), portrays the road in vertical strips showing the mileage, bridges, churches and towns en-route. It also marks the position of the gallows in each county and, in Meirionnydd; these were built just north of Harlech Castle.

Thomas Taylor's map of the counties of Wales entitled *An Exact Description of the Principality of Wales*, printed in 1718, distinctly shows a road running in a northwesterly direction that crosses over Llawllech ridge to Llanfair on the coast in the '*Meirioneth County Map*'.

Old London to Harlech road

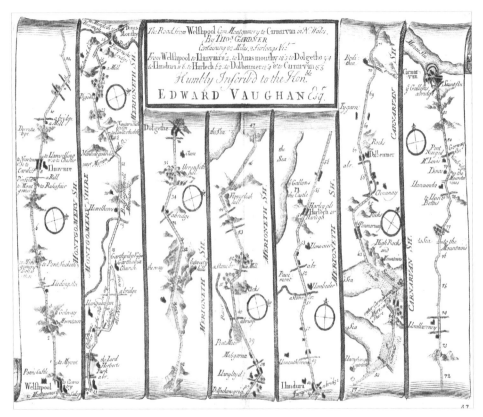

Early Travellers

The earliest record I have discovered of travellers who may have taken this route was in 1188. Baldwin, Archbishop of Canterbury, and Geraldus Cambrensis (Gerald of Wales) toured Wales trying to drum up support for the Crusades – their expedition around Wales is documented in *Gerald of Wales – The Journey Through*

Wales translated by Lewis Thorpe. Their journey took them northeast from Tywyn on the west coast up to Llanfair near Harlech. They crossed the Mawddach by rowing boat, with the horses swimming across, probably near Penmaenpool.

They were met on the north bank of the river and led onward by Gruffudd ap Cynan. Geraldus writes: '*This territory of Cynan, and especially Meirioneth, is the rudest and roughest of all the Welsh districts. The mountains are very high with narrow ridges and a great number of very sharp peaks all jumbled together in confusion and the men carry very large spears*'. Despite the inhospitable terrain, this was the shortest distance between Tywyn and Llanfair at the time by over two miles and therefore was the most likely route taken in order to complete their journey within a single day.

A Military Road

The road would have been extremely busy during the time of the rebuilding of Harlech Castle, which is thought to have taken place between 1283 and 1324. In the reign of Edward 1, hundreds of tradesmen and tons of materials, including military equipment for the garrison, would have been transported to the site by road and sea. Otto Grandison, a captain of Edward I, led 560 infantrymen over the mountains to Harlech after his capture of Castell y Bere on the Dysynni river in April 1283.

Money (in gold) to pay for the construction work on Harlech Castle was kept at Cymer Abbey near Dolgellau and was regularly transported over to Harlech to pay the bills.

John Owen Clenennau, Commander of a Royalist battalion during the Second Civil War, followed this route repeatedly in 1647 as he fled back and forth through Dyfryn Ardudwy hounded by a small force of Roundheads under the leadership of Twistleton Owen. (*Atlas Meirionnydd*)

Engraving: Harlech Castle by H Bartlett

"The Fat Welsh Knight!"

This story is not specifically about our particular road (it does feature a little bit!) but it is such a fascinating one that I felt I had to include it! Richard Vaughan, proprietor of Corsygedol, was elected MP for Meirioneth in 1628. In an article *Too Big to Ride he had to be Carried*, written by Frank Marriott, he states – '*He was so obese that a horse heavy enough to take him over the mountains just couldn't be found, so he had to be carried by sedan chair, or possibly a litter. He was carried in relays of four, or perhaps even six, perspiring and tired men*'. His tenants had to carry him miles from Corsygedol, over the Bwlch y Rhiwgyr pass and down to Mallwyd on the Welshpool road before he could travel by coach to London. This 'chore' is thought to have been part of their tenancy agreement.

On arrival at the House of Commons, both the double doors into the House had to be opened for him because of his size (special dispensation had to be granted as only the Black Rod was normally allowed to enter this way). The call would go out "*Here comes the fat Welsh Knight!*" as he entered the House. He died in 1636 from complications resulting from an operation

to remove some of his fat – surgeons being brought from London for the job.

Travellers on Foot

19th century miners, who lived near the coast, walked this route to the manganese mines in the Rhinogydd and the Dolgellau Gold Belt mines situated above Bont-ddu. Rain or shine, they would walk to work carrying all their own food early on Monday, stay in barracks during the working week, and return home the following Saturday afternoon (more about this in a later chapter on mining.)

A more recent traveller was Janet Haigh who died in 1953 aged 84. Her son Mervyn, Bishop of Winchester, had this memorial to her, made of local slate, placed by the track as it leaves Pont

top: Cymer Abbey; below: Corsygedol

AND S... ...NTS
STILL LOVE... ...THIS WAY
FROM TALYBONT TO PENMAENPOOL
THIS STONE
WAS PLACED IN 1953
BY HER SON MERVYN SOMETIME
BISHOP OF WINCHESTER

COURAGE TRAVELLER

The 'Post Boys'

Letters were carried by 'post boys' between towns and it is likely that the Vaughans of Corsygedol would have made use of this service. During their terms of office as 'Sheriff and MP for Meirioneth' during the 16th and 17th centuries they would have needed to communicate with Harlech, the seat of government at that time. Herbert Williams writes in *Stage Coaches in Wales* – *'These 'boys' were usually men of about 60 years old who were poorly paid and so badly mounted that their average speed was only four miles an hour. They were unarmed and easy prey for thieves and the Post Office actually advised customers not to send bank notes in one piece; they were cut in two with each piece being sent by different posts'*.

Scethin alongside her favourite walk.

> *'Gogoniant i Dduw (Glory to God)*
> *To the enduring memory of Janet Haigh*
> *who even as late as her eighty-fourth year*
> *despite dim sight and stiffened joints*
> *still loved to walk this way*
> *from Talybont to Penmaenpool'*

Janet must have been a fit lady for her years to tackle this tough, steep route that I find hard enough at my 'youthful' age!

top: Janet Haigh memorial;
below: Feral horses

Transportation

Various modes of transport such as packhorse, horse-drawn sled and ox-driven cart would have been used to carry goods to and from market and also bringing peat down from the mountains along this route.

One of the maps in Shirley Toulson's book *The Drovers' of North Wales* depicts the route from Dolgellau to Harlech and she calls it the '*old coach road*'. Herbert Williams writes in *Stage Coaches in Wales* – '*The first coaches were fairly crude and little better than covered wagons, generally drawn by four horses. Without suspension they could only travel at around 5 miles an hour on the rutted tracks and unmade roads of the time and during cold or wet weather, travel was often impossible*'. Travel by small, private coach could well have been possible over this difficult road in summer and dry weather.

It is unlikely, however, that the big stagecoaches of the time would have followed this route: Pont Scethin was probably too narrow to accommodate the wide axles and also the steep, zigzag climb

below: Horse drawn sled; next page: London to Harlech road

up to Llawllech ridge, followed by the high traverse around the Braich would have been extremely dangerous for these top-heavy coaches, especially in strong wind. This section of the road gradually fell out of regular use at the time when Dolgellau took over from Harlech as the centre of government in Meirionnydd and the Dolgellau to Barmouth road was improved in the late 1700s.

After hours of extensive research in archives and books I have found no record of any stagecoach service along this particular part of the road. One of the first stagecoach services in Meirionnydd, called 'The Wonder', was famous for its efficiency and time keeping and its earliest route in Meirionnydd ran between Mallwyd (near Dinas Mawddwy on the way to Welshpool) and Corwen in 1775.

Advertisements for coach services in the early 1800s claimed: '*Peculiar attractions to Tourists, as it commands some of the finest, most picturesque scenery and the fine views of Snowdonian Mountains, Bardsey Island, Harlech, Cader Idris, etc.*' – *Stage Coaches in Wales.*

below: Route over Llawllech ridge; opposite: Marker stone on old road

Rhinogydd: Ancient Routes and Old Roads

Visiting Tourists

Daniel Defoe (of *Robinson Crusoe* fame) visited Meirionnydd during his tour in 1725 and writes in *A Tour through England and Wales Volume II*: '*There is but few large towns in all this part, nor is it very populous; indeed much of it is scarcely habitable, but 'tis said, there are more sheep in it, than in all the rest of Wales. On the seashore, however, we see Harleigh-Castle, which is still a garrison and kept for the guard of the coast*'.

It was not until 1833, when the Barmouth Turnpike Road was built, that access by stagecoach to Barmouth from Dolgellau was possible. Barmouth became a favourite destination – a 'place to take the waters' – for the Victorian well-to-do, and notable people of the time, such as the poets Shelley and Byron, came seeking the magnificent mountain scenery. Some adventurous souls even climbed Cader Idris on foot or horseback accompanied by local guides.

The renowned Welsh landscape painter, Richard Wilson (1713–1782), who is said to have inspired Constable and Turner, produced beautiful stylized

below: Stage coach;
opposite: London to Harlech old road

paintings of Cader Idris. John Ruskin, the famous patron-of-the-arts and poet, was moved to write the following about the valley of the Mawddach when visiting in the 1870s:

"There is no better walk than from Barmouth through to Dolgellau other than from Dolgellau to Barmouth". This was a man who had visited the Alps and the Lake District – he obviously had impeccable taste!

The fortunes of Barmouth changed dramatically with the coming of the Cambrian Coast Railway from Machynlleth to Pwllheli in 1867. It developed quickly from a small fishing village and port, from where woollen goods made in Dolgellau were exported in the 18th century, into a busy coastal tourist resort.

My Favourite Walk

A walk I have undertaken many times, and one of my favourites, begins by parking at the top of a narrow road up from Bont-ddu. Go through the gate in the corner of the wall and follow an extremely rocky zigzag track up to a big marker stone. Take

below: Cader Idris;
opposite: Mawddach estuary

the right-hand fork at the junction and keep following the Braich ridge uphill to the top of Llawllech ridge on Diffwys where you can get fantastic panoramic views of the whole of the Yscethin valley and Snowdonia on a clear day.

Then turn west, face towards the sea and walk along the ridge beside a high wall until you join the top of Bwlch y Rhiwgr pass where it comes up from the Yscethin valley. Go left through the gate and, with Cader Idris directly ahead, follow the steep, rocky pass down to the left (the right-hand path goes down to Barmouth), go past the old healing well – great place for a picnic! – cross a small stone bridge over a tumbling stream coming down off the ridge and walk past a ruined barn back to the big marker stone at the junction of the two tracks.

This quite strenuous walk of about 5 ½ miles should take approximately 3-4 hours depending on your pace and fitness. You will need good, strong boots and carry waterproof clothing, appropriate OS Map and compass plus food and drink – have a safe journey!

left: Pont Scethin;
right: Old gate post

The Drovers

I have been exploring the drovers' roads that cross this part of Meirionnydd for many years and it has been a sheer delight to follow in the footsteps of the countless men and beasts that travelled these mountainous routes on their journey through to England.

Spending hours researching in books and the Meirionnydd Archives of Bangor, Caernarfon and Dolgellau about the drovers has been a profoundly fascinating experience. A list of archives and books I consulted can be found at the back of this volume if you wish to discover more about this amazing subject.

A Short History

Droving is thought to have started between Wales and England during Roman times when the Romans began to raise taxes, or 'tribute' as it was called, and payment in kind with slaves, metals such

Painting by J C Reed
'Drovers Near Beddgelert' 1863

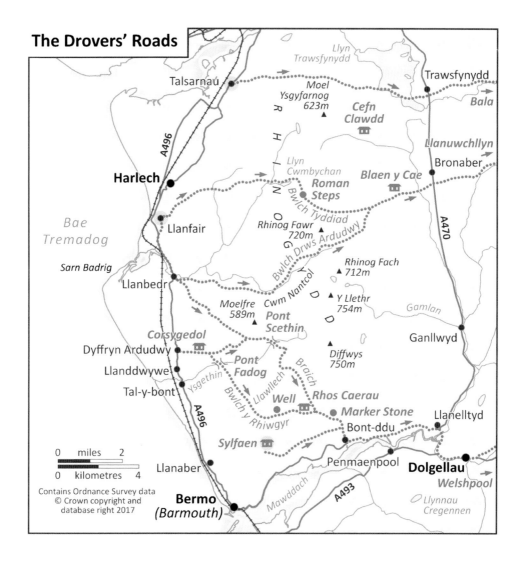

The Drovers' Roads

Talsarnau

Llyn Trawsfynydd

Trawsfynydd

Bala

Moel Ysgyfarnog 623m ▲

Cefn Clawdd

Llanuwchllyn

Bronaber

Harlech

Bae Tremadog

Llanfair

Llyn Cwmbychan

Roman Steps

Blaen y Cae

A470

Sarn Badrig

Rhinog Fawr 720m ▲

Bwlch Tyddiad

Bwlch Drws Ardudwy

Llanbedr

Rhinog Fach ▲ 712m

Cwm Nantcol

Y Llethr ▲ 754m

Gamlan

Moelfre 589m ▲

Pont Scethin

Corsygedol

Dyffryn Ardudwy

Diffwys 750m ▲

Ganllwyd

Llanddwywe

Pont Fadog

Braich

Ysgethin

Llawllech

Rhos Caerau

Llanelltyd

Tal-y-bont

Bwlch y Rhiwgyr

● Well

● *Marker Stone*

A496

Sylfaen

Bont-ddu

Llanaber

Penmaenpool

Dolgellau

0 miles 2
0 kilometres 4

Contains Ordnance Survey data © Crown copyright and database right 2017

Bermo (Barmouth)

Mawddach

A493

Welshpool

Llynnau Cregennen

as gold, copper or lead, and sometimes cattle was made.

There was a small trade before the 15th century but the Vagrancy Laws of the time made things difficult for Welsh drovers entering England. Trade between Wales and England improved after Henry VII rewarded his Welsh nobility for their support at the Battle of Bosworth, and many of these laws were rescinded.

The great increase in the population of London in the 16th century created a demand for meat that could not be met locally. By the mid 17th century the Welsh economy had become dependent on the cattle trade to England and it was well established by the time of the Civil War (1640–49).

Welsh farmers did not eat their own beef. Jackson, a young gentleman visiting the area in the late 18th century, commented in a letter to the Countess of Fingal that it was impossible to buy beef in Dolgellau at that time since "*all the cattle hereabouts are bought by drovers to send to England*". Poor people in those days made do with a very simple diet; it was found in 1794 by the newly formed Board of Agriculture that hard-working farmers existed on '*barley bread, oats, potatoes and bacon*' (Shirley Toulson – *The Drovers' Roads of Wales*).

After the coming of the railways to western Meirionnydd in the 1860s, the walking of cattle and other animals to the train terminals and local markets was still prevalent in more remote areas. The traditional old drove routes are still used to move sheep from the uplands of Dinas Mawddwy and western Montgomeryshire in the autumn to overwinter on lowland farms along the coast of Ardudwy near Harlech; the sheep would make the return journey in the spring.

The Drovers' Routes

As shown on the Route Map, there were a number of routes taken by the drovers from this part of Meirionnydd in an easterly direction through the mountains. The more northerly routes led towards Bala and on to Llangollen; the southerly routes led down to Dolgellau and on to Welshpool. These are ancient strategic route-ways used long before the time of the drovers and were the most direct for travelling inland at the time.

The northern-most route on the Map,

opposite: Cwm Nantcol; next page: Drws Ardudwy

that traversed the top end of the Rhinogydd range, passed through land now flooded when Llyn Trawsfynydd was expanded in 1924 to supply water for Maentwrog Hydroelectric Power Station.

In the central region, two main routes traversed from west to east over rocky mountain passes. One is via Cwm Bychan and over Bwlch Tyddiad and the other is via Cwm Nantcol and Bwlch Drws Ardudwy over to Bronaber – both are extremely steep and rocky.

Maes y Garnedd, a farm in Cwm Nantcol, was the home of Colonel John Jones, nephew to Oliver Cromwell. Jones was one of the judges at the trial of King Charles I and a signatory on the King's death warrant. After the ascension of Charles II, he was impeached for high treason and executed in 1660.

Further south, one of the more regularly used routes from the west coast was Bwlch y Rhiwgyr pass. This route met up with the old London-to-Harlech road by a large milestone before heading south down to Bont-ddu and on to Dolgellau.

A retainer of Robert Evans' father of

below: Llyn Trawsfynydd;
opposite: Bwlch Tyddiad drovers' route

Rhinogydd: Ancient Routes and Old Roads

Rhiwgyr pass, was renowned for curing skin abnormalities. I was sitting here having lunch one day, when a magnificent hare bounded down the mountain to drink at the well; he spotted me and we regarded each other for a few seconds before he turned and sped away – a special moment!

The Drove

From spring through to September small black cattle, called 'runts' aged between 18 months and three years of age, would be gathered at specific points or collected enroute from smaller farms. They would be driven from dawn to dusk at an average of 2 miles an hour and the drove would generally cover 12 to 15 miles a day, though much less over the more mountainous passes. It would take about three weeks for the whole journey of roughly 250-300 miles over some of the most difficult and dangerous terrain in the UK (Twm Elias).

Sylfaen Farm told him that 'criminals' would be chained to the cattle in Harlech to be taken for trial at the Welshpool Assizes. They would be imprisoned overnight in cells near Rhos Caerau, an overnight stopping place above Barmouth, while the drovers went to the pub! He can remember as a child, seeing the iron rings where the men were shackled – they have long since rusted away.

An ancient healing well (Ffynnon Iachau), situated at the bottom of Bwlch y

It was important to keep the cattle calm as the Welsh Blacks had a tendency to panic; they were extremely agile and fast runners. Driving the beasts over such hard terrain called for great skills and experience and the drovers could not afford to be cruel as the cattle needed to

top left: Cells at Caerau; bottom left: Rhos Caerau; above: Ffynnon Iachau

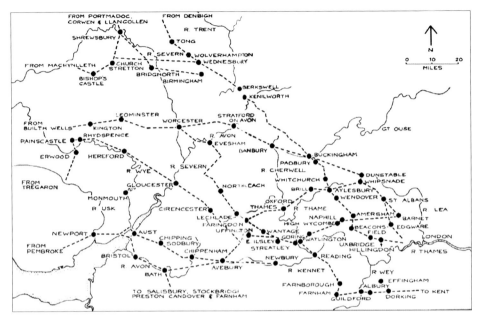

arrive in good condition. The trick was to deliver the beasts in better condition than when they started and if they were driven at their own pace, and fed well en-route, the exertion of the journey would enable them to build up muscle. The cattle also fattened quickly on the rich English pastures they passed through.

The cattle did well even on poor mountain pasture and there is an old joke that they could put on fat eating just the twine tied around the hay bales on their winter-feed. The value of these mountain cattle was that they gained weight more quickly than any other breed once they were put on good pasture and for this reason they were in great demand in England.

above: Drovers' routes through England;
opposite: Bwlch y Rhiwgyr pass

The average size of a drove would be about 80-100 cattle and for the first few days they would be extremely lively and noisy before settling down to a steady pace. The head drover, or one of his men, would set off on horseback half an hour before the drove to check out the safety of the route ahead. They would yell 'Heip-trrrrw Ho!' to pre-warn farmers to safeguard their cattle from being swept up into the herd (Twm Elias).

The drover would have 2-3 helpers and their dogs to control the animals, this was especially important passing through

above: Llannerch-y-medd;
opposite: Welsh Black bull

villages and when meeting other droves. One or two of the men would be regular employees while others were tough 'men of the road', well able to overnight with the animals for protection. The drover, therefore, had to be not only a good cattleman but also an astute businessman when dealing with the hard-bargaining farmers and also when selling to cattle buyers. He also needed to be able to take care of himself on the return journey when carrying the cattle sale money.

Good communication between the men was extremely important for keeping control of the drove and a series of special whistles and calls were used. It must have been a nerve-wracking experience for travellers coming face-to-face with this mass of cattle on the road!

Drovers sometimes stopped at Barnet en-route to trade in horses and a few cattle. Most of the cattle droves from north Wales went firstly to Chelmsford in Essex or to Kent where the cattle were fattened prior to being driven to Smithfield Market in London. According to Teri Brewer in *The Welsh Drovers* – '*in 1625 as many as 60,000 cattle a year left*

Wales for London and by 1851, 277,000 Welsh cattle made the trip as well as a million sheep'.

The larger and stronger Welsh Blacks of Anglesea were regarded as particularly suitable for ploughing and, for centuries, there was a steady trade with Sussex farmers (*Life and Tradition in Rural Wales* – J Geraint Jenkins).

The Journey

To aid navigation, scots pines were planted as landmarks along the routes at strategic points on high ground and were also used as an indicator for an overnight stopping place at a farmhouse or inn. The head drover would stay in the accommodation with the rest of the men bedding down with the cattle or in a barn if available. The cattle were corralled in *ha'penny fields*; so-called as this was the overnight charge per beast.

As well as food and accommodation, entertainment of various kinds such as dancing, music – harpists were popular – poetry and storytelling was supplied at the inns. Wrestling matches between drovers and farmers were often held. Orig

Scots pines on drovers' route; opposite: Blaen y Cae farm

Williams, the world-renowned professional wrestler from Ysbyty Ifan, claims he was from a long tradition of wrestlers dating back to drovers in the Conwy valley (Twm Elias).

On the return journey, the drovers were 'the newspapers of the day' and they were relied upon for spreading both national and international news from village to village. The British victory at the Battle of Waterloo in 1815 was passed on in this way. They were a mine of information and gossip; tips about agricultural practices, tales of gruesome murders, swearwords and even music-hall tunes, some of which became adapted as popular Welsh hymn tunes, were brought back by the drovers.

It was from the drovers that, in the 18th century, struggling farmers heard of the easy riches to be had in America and many young people from rural Wales made the decision to seek their fortune in this 'land of opportunity'.

For safety reasons, people would often travel to London with the drovers. Shirley Toulson writes that, by the 18th century, the sons of rich landowners wishing to go

left: Bwlch y Rhiwgyr drovers' route;
right: Blaen y Cae farm

to London would ride along with the drovers for the adventure. Men taking up posts in England would often sign on as temporary helpers, young men beginning apprenticeships in the City of London and girls on their way to work as maids in the London houses, or as seasonal fruit-sellers on the streets, would also accompany them.

Shoeing the Cattle

Cattle and horses had to be carefully shod before the long journey and shoes – called cues – frequently had to be renewed en-route. Wear and tear on the animals' feet, if not treated, was potentially disastrous, affecting their condition and reducing the pace. Blacksmiths often travelled with the droves to be available when needed.

The beast had to be thrown and roped prior to shoeing and the speed and skill with which this was done was remarkable. A strong man was required to do this job. It is recorded that one farrier and his assistant could shoe well over a hundred beasts in a day (Philip Gwyn Hughes – *Wales and the Drovers*).

Robin Gof, born 1814, an experienced cattle-shoeing blacksmith from

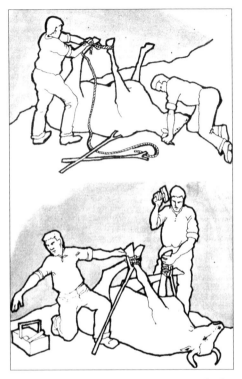

Trawsfynydd, went many times with the droves to England. He would have spent much of the winter producing hundreds of pairs of cues ready for the spring droves.

above: Shoeing cattle by Anne Lloyd Cooper;
opposite: Pont Fadog on drovers' route

Gof was an exceptionally strong man and in a fight would only need to strike once (Merched y Wawr – *A History of Trawsfynydd*). On one occasion, he knocked out a thief who had waylaid him on the road home from one of his trips. He thought he had killed the man and he fled to France. Some years later he met someone in Paris who informed him that his assailant was alive and well so he returned home and was one of the few men in north Wales fluent in French.

Llety Lloegr, a cottage strategically

above: Llety Lloegr shoeing station;
below: Cattle (cues) shoes

placed at the bottom of Bwlch y Rhiwgyr, housed an emergency shoeing station and was the last inn for the drovers before their tough journey over the high pass. It is a holiday cottage now and is situated near Pont Fadog on the Corsygedol Estate.

The Drovers (**Porthmyn**)

During the reign of Elizabeth 1, droving became a licensed profession and, to qualify, the drover would need to be male, over 30, married and a landowner and able to speak reasonable English. Licensing was supposed to eliminate undesirable characters who, in the past, would often abscond with the money – Ireland being a favourite destination. Droving without a license incurred large fines and imprisonment for breaking the Vagrancy Law. The biggest crime of all was to move cattle on the Sabbath and again huge fines and imprisonment were rigorously enforced. Droving under the influence of alcohol was also illegal and, in 1872, the fine was 40 shillings or one month in jail. A further law in Queen Ann's reign made it impossible for a drover to declare himself bankrupt as a way of freeing himself from any obligation he had undertaken.

Here are two pertinent verses taken

from a long poem written by Rhys Pritchard, a Vicar, (1549–1644) informing drovers of the correct code of behaviour.

Cynngor I'r Porthmon

Os 'dwyt borthmon dela'n onest,
Tal yn gywir am y gefaist;
Cadw d'air, na thorr addewid;
Gwell nag aur mewn cod yw credid.

Gochel feddwi wrth borthmonna,
Gwin hel borthmon i gardotta;
Os y porthmon a fydd meddw,
Fa'r holl stoc i brynu'r cwrw

Advice to Drovers

If you are a drover, deal honestly,
Pay a fair price for what you have
Keep your word, do not break promises,
Better than gold, is a code of ethics.

Beware of drinking while you're droving
Wine will reduce the drover to a beggar,
If the drover is a drunkard,
All his stock will buy his beer.

The senior drovers were mounted on sturdy horses and the breed most commonly used was the traditional Welsh Cob. The horses would often be sold in London and the drovers travelled back by coach or on foot. This breed has been in existence throughout Wales for many

below: Grave of Richard Jarrett, Drover; right: Sylvanus Evans, Drover following page: Cefn Clawdd old farm

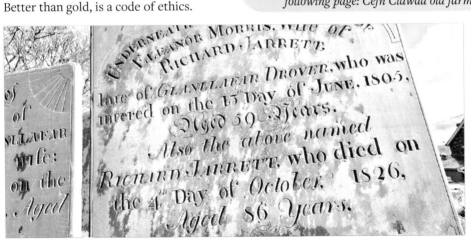

centuries and feral horses can still be found on the east side of the Rhinogydd. Robert Evans says that, in his father's day, wild horses were rounded up, corralled on Sylfaen Farm and starved for a while in order to make it easier to break them in.

Local Drovers

Sylvanus Evans (1833–1911) was a well-known drover and horse-dealer from Blaenau Ffestiniog and William Roland, who kept a tavern in Maentwrog in 1762, was described as '*a topsman drover*' *and a dealer of considerable standing and of unassailable integrity*'. Rowland Edmund, a drover and farmer, also from Maentwrog, left a personal estate of £963 in 1819 – a substantial amount of money in those days (*The Drovers of Snowdonia* – Snowdonia National Park article). The grave of Richard Jarrett, Drover who died in 1826 aged 86, lies in St Madryn's churchyard in Trawsfynydd.

Drovers' Apparel

Drovers worked under very difficult conditions and clothing had to be suitable for all weathers. Shirley Toulson writes that the clothing they wore remained much the same throughout the centuries. '*A wide-brimmed felt hat made from mulching tree bark and hemp, with both trousers and a cape made from wool and hemp. Underwear was pure wool. Clogs were soled with Alder as this does not rot. To keep out the wet, trousers were protected by knee-length woollen*

stockings bought from the weekly stocking fair in Bala. The whole leg would then be covered in old-fashioned Bristol brown paper, animal fat applied and finally the whole leg tied over with leather thongs' (probably more effective than Gortex today but a trifle smellier!) Soap was applied to the soles of the stockings to help avoid blistering from friction. This soap would contain excessive amounts of lanolin from the wool grease – very different to modern highly refined soap. Lanolin is an essential component of today's expensive skin-care products.

In 1953, the Everest Expedition wore long Welsh woollen stockings and also used the technique of applying soap to the feet to prevent friction. Dr Charles Evans, in charge of the expedition, heard of this tip when conversing with shepherds during their training in the Snowdonia mountains.

Drovers' Pay

The drovers earned good pay. Usually this would be 10% of the sales money, but expenses would be high: overnight pasture for the animals, food and accommodation for the men, tollgates, etc. Professor

left: Tŷ Newydd farm buildings;
right: Old tannery

Caroline Skeel of the Royal Historical Society recorded that a 19th century drover from Dolgellau received three shillings a day. A weekly wage for the youngest drover was twice the going agricultural wage of the time and all food and drink was provided en-route, he was also given six shillings bonus at the end of each journey after the cattle were sold.

Cattle Dogs

One of the most popular dogs used by the drovers of south west Wales was the Cardigan or Pembrokeshire Corgi. They were extremely tough, hardy and aggressive by nature – so nimble that they could nip the heels of the cattle and short-legged enough to avoid being kicked.

A breed used more in north Wales was much larger, red in colour with strong legs, a bushy tail and looked rather like a large fox. Some people falsely believe that this similarity to a fox is a possible reason for its demise. The Welsh Sheepdog worked cattle in a different way to the black-and-white Scottish Border Collie that has since superseded it. The Welsh Sheepdog drives the animals instead of rounding them up and is currently undergoing a revival and becoming popular once again (Twm Elias).

After the sales in London were complete, the assistants' dogs would be

Cardiganshire Working Corgi;
opposite: Mab

Rhinogydd: Ancient Routes and Old Roads

sent home; it seems they had an unsurpassed homing instinct and were able to retrace their outward route and stay in the same overnight places where their 'keep' had already been paid for. There is a tradition in the Harlech district that when the dogs eventually arrived home, the wives knew that their men would not be far behind.

First Aid

The drovers would equip themselves with the equivalent of a 'first aid kit'. Chewing lumps of 'bacci', called 'Twist', was reported to help the drovers survive the rigors of the long journey. Dark brown in colour, the thickness of a pencil and coiled like a rope, it was used as a general

painkiller. Unfortunately it left dreadful staining on the teeth but seemed to work as a protection for the gums (Idris Evans – *The Hard Road to London*).

If men suffered cuts to any part of their body the dogs would be encouraged to lick the wounds as the saliva was thought to act as an antiseptic. The wound would then be covered with a hemp leaf and bound to keep out dirt. The fact that many of the drovers survived to a great age suggests that continued exposure to the elements and countless nights sleeping in the open air had no permanent adverse

Thomas Rowland 1797
'Llangothen Hill in the road of Ruthin'

effects upon their health although some were not so fortunate and died of pneumonia (Richard Moore-Colyer – *Welsh Cattle Drovers*).

Dangers

There were many hazards to be overcome on their long journey over the difficult terrain and mountain passes. Wolves were a hazard and known to exist in the Rhinogydd area up to the 15th century. Thieves were a constant threat too as it was generally known that drovers were often entrusted to transport money to London for businessmen and the Exchequer. They also carried their own expenses for the journey and, on their return transported large sums of money from the cattle sales. The thickly forested Welsh border areas and dense wooded roads into Essex were infested with highwaymen.

Secret compartments were sometimes built into the saddles and their clothes and used for concealment of the gold coins

below: Rhinog Fach;
opposite: Drws Arduddwy

Rhinogydd: Ancient Routes and Old Roads

collected by local officials to pay the Ship Tax. Drovers delivered this tax to the London Exchequer as late as the mid 18th century and they earned a good commission from it. This tax had to be paid from the time of Charles 1 if one owned a dwelling from where a ship could be seen at sea. The money collected was supposed to have been spent on building ships for the defence of the coast. I am relieved this tax has been abolished because I would be liable to pay this tax today due to the beautiful view of Cardigan Bay from my house!

Banking

Increasing commerce and the need for safety in transporting large sums of money (the sale of a drove of a hundred cattle would raise about £800 in the early 1800s) was a powerful impetus for the

below: Promissory bank note;
opposite: Oak fencepost on drovers' route

development of the early banking system. Once the monopoly of the Bank of England was broken in the mid 1700s, many local banking companies were set up which offered a service to trades in particular areas, eg banks for shipping in coastal towns.

In Wales, and nowhere else in Britain, two banks were established in the late 18th century to service the needs of drovers. One was the Black Sheep Bank of Aberystwyth and Tregaron and the other the Black Ox Bank of Llanymddyfri. The Black Sheep Bank issued banknotes depicting one black sheep (£1), two black sheep (£2) and a black ram (£5) and the Black Ox Bank notes showed a black ox.

The Black Horse bank was started by the Lloyd family of Dolobran in Montgomeryshire mostly servicing manufacturing in the English Midlands; Lloyds Bank (still using The Sign of the Black Horse) eventually took over The Black Ox Bank in 1909 (Twm Elias).

The notes supplied by these early banks could not be used for buying goods but acted as 'promissory notes' and only be exchanged for money by the recognized account holder in one of the bank's branches. This meant that under this

arrangement, if the notes were stolen, they could not be cashed. The system worked whereby the drover, in London or Barnet, took the cash from selling his cattle to a local bank that had an arrangement to issue notes on behalf of the drovers' banks, each one would be dated, numbered and signed. Ceredigion Museum in Aberystwyth has one of the original Black Sheep Bank notes on display. The statement *"I Promise to pay the Bearer the Sum of ... On Demand"* written on these early notes can still be found on our bank notes today.

Blaen y Cae

Blaen y Cae farm lies at the start of Bwlch Tyddiad Pass near Bronaber and three Scots pines can still be seen by the house that marked its use as an overnight stopping place for the drovers. It is now only used to store hay. On the south side there is a large walled pasture where the grass is noticeably much greener than the surrounding land. The richness of the grass is mainly due to years of fertilization by hundreds of cattle penned here overnight – a giveaway sign for a *ha'penny field*.

Blaen y Cae

I have sat beneath the Scots pines by the farmhouse and imagined what it must have been like when the drovers arrived here – the noise of men whistling and shouting, dogs barking and sounds of cattle settling for the night.

In my journeying through the Rhinogydd, I have come across a number of abandoned hill farms that have now fallen into ruin that once supported a unique way of life. I wonder how much longer it will be before hill farming in the Rhinogydd passes into history forever.

Blaen y Cae

Mines of Meirionnydd

It is virtually impossible to walk in the uplands of Meirionnydd without coming across the remains of industrial buildings and waste tips from derelict mines and quarries and I have spent hours exploring what is left of these old workings. The land has been mined for gold, manganese, copper, lead, zinc and slate over the years but only a few made a large profit – Mark Twain described a mine as "*a hole in the ground owned by a liar*".

Experts in this field say that if it is metal that is produced it is defined as a mine whereas slate is always from a quarry regardless of whether it is opencast or underground.

In the 1800s, when these industries were at their peak, there would have been hundreds of men living and working across this vast mountainous area. Due to the remoteness of most of the mines, they would travel to begin work early Monday morning and not return home until Saturday afternoon; living in communal barracks on site during the week. This was a tough and dangerous occupation but, at the time, little other work was available and it was much better paid than agricultural labouring.

Gold Mines

The reason most people have heard about Welsh Gold is its use in the wedding rings of Royalty including, most recently, for the marriage of Catherine Middleton to Prince William in 2011. Other special Royal Regalia has been fashioned from Welsh Gold including the crown for George, Prince of Wales, and later King George V, for his investiture at Caernarfon Castle in 1901, which was sourced from a gold mine near Trawsfynydd. Doug Lennox states in *Now You Know: Royalty*. '*When the former King Edward VIII (son of George V) went into exile as the Duke of Windsor in 1936 following his abdication, he took with him the Coronet of George, Prince of Wales worn at his Investiture – a highly controversial act!*' – It was returned after the Duke's death and now resides in St James' Palace, London but many Welsh people feel it should be displayed in Wales.

The mines run in a band along the north of the Mawddach called The Dolgellau Gold Belt and they have been

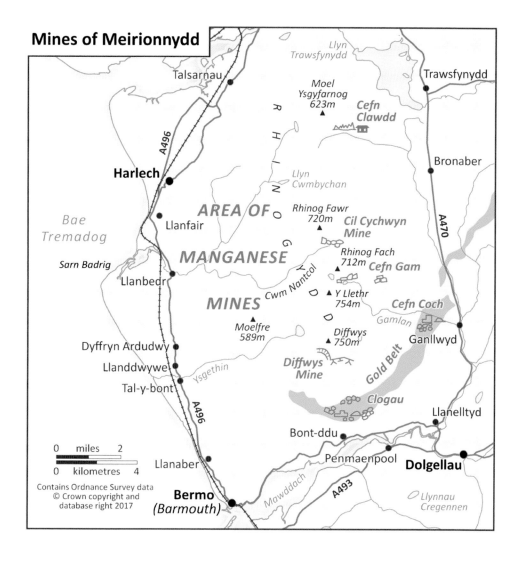

Mines of Meirionnydd

Talsarnau

Llyn Trawsfynydd

Trawsfynydd

Moel Ysgyfarnog 623m ▲

Cefn Clawdd

RHINOG

Bronaber

A470

Harlech

Bae Tremadog

Llanfair

Llyn Cwmbychan

AREA OF

Rhinog Fawr 720m ▲

Cil Cychwyn Mine

MANGANESE

Rhinog Fach 712m ▲

Cefn Gam

Sarn Badrig

Llanbedr

Cwm Nantcol

Y Llethr 754m ▲

Cefn Coch

Gamlan

MINES

Moelfre 589m ▲

Diffwys 750m ▲

Ganllwyd

Dyffryn Ardudwy

Diffwys Mine

Gold Belt

Llanddwywe

Tal-y-bont

Ysgethin

Clogau

Llanelltyd

A496

Bont-ddu

0 miles 2

0 kilometres 4

Llanaber

Penmaenpool

Dolgellau

Contains Ordnance Survey data © Crown copyright and database right 2017

Bermo (Barmouth)

Mawddach

A493

Llynnau Cregennen

worked intermittently from early times with varying degrees of success. T A Morris writes in *Merionethshire*: '*The Romans knew of the presence of gold in the quartz of the Ganllwyd. Mixed with the flux from smelting-furnaces were several pieces of pottery of Roman make*'.

At one time, there were at least 24 gold mines operating in the Gold Belt. Very few of the smaller ones ever produced any return for their investment but money earned from them was a bonus for the local economy. According to H J Owen in *The Treasures of the Mawddach* – '*When the mines were working, the Mawddach Valley buzzed with life and excitement. Hundreds of men were engaged, most of whom spent their earnings at Dolgelley, thereby enriching many of the local tradesmen*'.

In the 19th century, there were three gold rushes in Meirionnydd, in 1853–4, 1862 and 1887 but mining continued up to the First World War and in a small way afterwards. C J Williams reports in *Metal Mines of North Wales* – '*A total of 126,340 oz of gold was recovered from 279,027 tons of ore between 1861 and 1938 with peak production in 1904 of 19,655 oz*'.

T H Roberts was a gold prospector and supplier of all things for mining and, when he died in the 1990s, the shop was still chock-full of mining gear (his hardware shop in Dolgellau is now a splendid café and still contains the original wooden fittings). In 1890, whilst prospecting on the side of Y Garn, men hired by him found two small metallic objects covered in dirt, later identified as a unique silver-gilt Chalice and Paten from Cymer Abbey. It is thought they had been hidden when Henry VIII was sacking the monasteries of their wealth in the mid 1500s, to be retrieved at a later date. According to H J Owen in his book *The Treasures of the*

Clogau Gold Mine

Rhinogydd: Ancient Routes and Old Roads

Mawddach, the Chalice was made in the 13th century and "*Nicholas de Hereford me Fecit*" – *Nicholas of Hereford made me* – is inscribed on it. They are now housed in the National Museum of Wales in Cardiff

On Mondays, men working at the mines had to carry all their food up to their accommodation for the week and they often resorted to local game to supplement their diet. Hugh Pugh, an installer of mine machinery in the late 1880s, who worked in many of the gold mines, wrote a poem on a postcard – it seems he was pretty sick of eating rabbit everyday for dinner:

> "*Rabbits young, rabbits old,*
> *Rabbits hot, rabbits cold,*
> *Rabbits tender, rabbits tough,*
> *Thank the Lord we had enough!*"

The mines are now silent and mostly due to their inaccessibility are not seen as viable business ventures at the present time. Rhododendrons and birch trees flourish amongst the waste tips and the ruined buildings have become sanctuaries for birds, animals and plants.

I have chosen two quite different gold mines to include here I have explored in depth. Clogau Mine is the most famous and the richest. It covered a vast area north of Bont-ddu and is relatively easy to explore. Whereas Cefn Coch Mine is small in comparison, produced little gold and is also much less accessible high up on the eastern side of Y Garn. What both mines have in common, however, are the fantastic views of the surrounding mountains in good visibility.

Clogau Gold Mine *SH 668 193*

Clogau is located high above the north side

below: Clogau Gold Mine – breaking quartz;
opposite: Clogau Gold Mine

of the Mawddach and the views of Diffwys and Cader Idris are superb. 'The mines consists of a large group of workings that covered a large area known as Mynydd Clogau (Clogau Mountain) and included, among others, St David's (the richest lode), Vigra and Old Clogau' (Metal Mines of North Wales). There are adits (mine entrances), ruined industrial buildings, bits of machinery and piles of quartz to investigate all over the mountain and I have paid frequent visits exploring what must have been a flourishing hub of industry.

Gold was first discovered here in 1834 but it was not until 1854 that a company was formed to work the mine. Brian Slyfield writes in Echoes of the Gold Rush by the Mawddach – 'An old spoil heap of quartz, initially abandoned as it did not contain copper, was found to be richly gold-bearing and it yielded many thousands of pounds worth of gold'.

H J Owen records in Treasures of the Mawddach – 'The excavated ore was broken up by hand and the gold-bearing quartz placed in a wooden chest and transferred to the britten pans for separation by Robin the

above: Gold mine truck;
below: Gold-bearing quartz;
opposite: Clogau Gold Mine workers

Donkey who was a great favourite with the miners. Robin, it is said, was a very miserable donkey over the weekend when the mine was deserted!'

The St David's Gold Cup, which is played for annually on the Royal St David's Golf Course in Harlech, was first competed for in 1904. It is thought to have been made from gold mined at Clogau (sometimes also called St David's Mine) and is so valuable that it is kept in the bank for 364 days of the year and only makes an annual appearance on the day of the final – Information: Richard Fisher.

Surviving bankruptcy in 1858, Clogau went on to eventually became the most productive and extensive mine in the area and, in just over three years, had produced gold to the value of £43,780. Its best year was 1904 when 14,000 tons of ore produced 18,400 oz of gold valued at about £3.16d per oz making a total of £58,000 (equivalent to over £6.5 million today!) At its peak 253 men, 190 underground and 63 surface workers, were employed at Clogau. The mine closed in 1910 but there are ongoing rumours of a possible reopening.

A range of jewellery containing Clogau gold can still be obtained from Clogau Gold of Wales Limited – a quote on their

website says "*Every piece we create contains rare Welsh gold – the Gold of Royalty for over 100 years*".

Cefn Coch Gold Mine *SH 713 224*

Also known as The New California Mine, it was not the most productive gold mine in the Gold Belt but, as with many mines and quarries, the view from its location high up on the southeast side of the Y Garn is captivating. On a clear day, Rhobell and the Arenig Mountains can be seen in the distance with the bulk of Y Garn looming above.

Similar to all the Meirionnydd gold

mines, most of the underground adits are fenced off for safety but a few at Cefn Coch can still be accessed with great care as the entrances are low and running with water. A well-preserved trackway leading to the remains of a caban (rest-house for the men) links one of the main adits to the ruins of a steam-driven mill building; nearby are two barracks that housed men during the week. A large number of old workings, adits and heaps of spoil can still be found winding up a steep bank leading towards Y Garn ridge.

Cefn Coch Gold Mine

G W Hall writes in *The Gold Mines of Meirioneth* – '*Gold was discovered here in 1862 and the total recorded output between 1862 and 1912 was 2,661 tones of ore producing 1,392 oz of gold. Its most successful year was 1894 when 360 tons of ore produced 180 oz of gold; it finally closed in 1914*'.

Slate Quarries

I have always had a passion for slate and exploring slate quarries. My first book, published in 1999, bi-lingual Welsh-English, was written about Rhosydd Slate Quarry positioned high above Tanygrisiau village near Blaenau Ffestiniog, so I just had to include one here.

Cefn Gam Slate Quarry SH 680 256

The first lease on the quarry, dated 1834, was awarded to Lewis Pugh, the Crown Agent for the Dolgellau area, who foresaw the opportunity to supply the growing town of Dolgellau with slate, undercutting Ffestiniog slate due to savings on transport costs.

Cefn Gam actually produced little in terms of slate but did generate a great number of court cases for such a small quarry including many for unpaid rents.

The saddest being that of George William Pybus whose involvement in Cefn Cam led him to bankruptcy in 1905 and probably an early grave in 1906 as a consequence (Information: Richard Williams).

Situated in the centre of a wide valley beneath Y Llethr and Rhinog Fach, Cefn Gam is one of the few slate quarries in this part of Meirionnydd. It is small in comparison with the Blaenau quarries and was mostly 'open air' extraction with little underground working. '*The slate was of a good colour, but although it did not readily split, it made a tough flexible product. Due to its remoteness there are a number of buildings still standing including a dressing shed, a workshop/office and a mill? There is a further building, possibly a barracks and a fine manager's house. The latter has a nice underground food store and the garden still shows evidence of careful cultivation*' writes Alun John Richards in *A Gazetteer of the Welsh Slate Industry*. The food store Alun mentions is still in a good state of repair and looks like an air-raid shelter filled with ferns growing out of the inner walls.

Accessing Cefn Gam requires a long walk through Cwm Mynach forest along an extremely wet track, but it is worth the

effort to explore the unique variety of buildings that still survive here due to its isolated position. On an earlier visit I made to the quarry, the mist came pouring down over the ridge and the wind swirled it around us like ghosts. This made for great atmospheric images but felt extremely spooky!

Manganese Mines

There are records of at least 50 manganese mines scattered around this part of Meirionnydd with a large number located high up in the Rhinogydd Mountains and on the cliffs of Diffwys. They were mainly very small enterprises – manganese was worked for only a short period at the end of the 19th century, with a bit of a revival during WWI. Most of the mining was undertaken under license but Cefn Clawdd Manganese Mine was worked by the farmer landowner.

Chris Down writes in *The Manganese Mines of North Wales* – 'In Meirionnydd, manganese was mined from around 1823 with the main periods of mining being 1835–1840, when outcrops were worked on near Barmouth, from 1884 to around 1900, when

all images left: Cefn Gam Slate Quarry; right: Diffwys Manganese Mine trackway

the major development of the Meirionnydd mines occurred, and during the First World War (1914–1918) *when a number of the mines reopened. Manganese has many uses but by far the main one was to improve the wear resistance and hardness of steel. At least 90% of world manganese ore production is used by the iron and steel industries.*

Manganese workings tend not to be as spectacular as gold and slate as they often just look like deep, rough furrows scoured along the edge of a track with rocks and earth piled up on either side. The following two I have chosen are located high up in cliffs on the Rhinogydd.

Diffwys Manganese Mine SH 669 238

Tucked beneath the summit of Diffwys at 600m, this mine is possibly the highest in Meirionnydd. *'Only open from 1886 to 1887, manpower in 1887 was 13 underground and 10 surface workers. Removing the ore from its difficult placement called for a series of tramways, inclines and an aerial ropeway needed to be built; at a lower point access was via a track through Cwm Mynach originally developed to serve the Cefn Gam Slate Quarry.'* Information: *The Welsh Mines Society*.

To access the mine requires a long, arduous slog up towards the ridge, the path initially runs through Cwm Mynach forest, then follows a series of steep inclines and trackways (some still in excellent condition) in order to reach the main workings located near the top of the mountain. Due to its inaccessibility, quite a few remnants of the workings mentioned in the Welsh Mines Society description can still be seen.

Cil Cychwyn Manganese Mine

SH 654 267

From its location on a steep cliff above

left: Iron ring Diffwys Mine; right: Cil Cychwyn Manganese Mine

Cwm Nantcol, you can see the winding Cwmnantcol river far below as it snakes down towards the sea; also visible are the distinct lines of an older river course running through a patchwork field system. *'The mine covers a considerable area situated along a cliff-face with the remains of buildings (a smithy, stable and barracks), tramways, tips and both old opencast and underground workings. Originally open from 1891 to 1894 (the year of its maximum output of 1,064 tons), it reopened in 1918 until 1920'* – The Welsh Mines Society.

Old workings and ruined buildings still exist high up along the cliff and access to the site is via a steep walk up a trackway visible from the road. Bwlch Tyddiad, the ancient road that passes between Rhinog Fawr and Rhinog Fach, can be seen below the mine in the valley. This route was used to bring building materials and weaponry across to Harlech Castle and was also taken by the drovers on their way east to Trawsfynydd.

Safety First

When visiting the mines, you will frequently see the faded danger signs depicting a man falling posted around the

below: Cil Cychwyn manganese mine; right: Manganese mine entrance; Warning sign

fenced-off entrances, and they are there for a good reason as old mines and quarries are full of potential hazards. Loose roofing slates lying on rotten wooden beams can descend like guillotines, especially if it is windy and I have seen slate walls blown over in a strong gust. A few years ago I fell through the floor of an old mill into an underground pit when rotten floorboards collapsed under my weight. Luckily I sustained only a few cuts and bruises and my camera survived too! So please take special care!

A Photographer's Paradise

During the years I have been exploring this wild and beautiful part of Meirionnydd I have experienced so many wonderful sights and sounds. One such captivating moment was in the high moorland of the Rhinogydd when I watched a splendid Marsh Harrier silently ranging back and forth over the tall grass searching for prey. This is the only time I have ever seen one anywhere as, unfortunately, it is an extremely rare bird in Wales. If you are lucky you may well see a Peregrine Falcon, that magnificent pursuer of hapless pigeons; hear the deep "cronk" of a Raven, and the three short whistles of a Ring Ouzel, slightly smaller than a blackbird with a beautiful white moon-shaped bib on its chest – another bird decreasing in numbers.

Whilst sound-recording in the Rhinogydd in 2013 I was lucky enough to capture the cry of a curlew that I included in the film for my final Masters Degree Assignment – Yr Hen Ffyrdd/The Old Ways. In the late spring the air is full of the song of skylarks marking out their aerial territory and I have never seen so many elsewhere. There is little disturbance for birds and other animals in this wild place and it is gratifying to see wildlife that is so under pressure elsewhere flourishing here – long may it remain so!

Lakes and Rivers

One thing that can be guaranteed here in the Rhinogydd is an abundance of water to fill the rivers and lakes! Many of the lakes in Meirionnydd have legends linked to them and the three I have chosen here are excellent examples in this tradition.

Llyn Cwmbychan SH 640 313

Llyn Cwmbychan nestles underneath the jagged cliffs of Carreg y Saeth and, like many Snowdonia lakes, bears a sad legend: Cadwgan, a local chieftain, had a daughter, Cilwen, who fell in love with a shepherd, Merwydd Ddu. But the match was heavily frowned upon and they were forbidden to meet. One day, after a storm had raged for three days, Merwydd's body was found on the shore of the lake. Poor Cilwen was

Llyn Cwmbychan

heartbroken and she was later found dead lying on his grave. They were buried together and the grave is marked with a cairn and a long slab of rock. It is claimed that sometimes they are seen walking arm-in-arm over the lake waters. (*The Lakes of Eryri* by Geraint Roberts).

Llyn Bodlyn *SH 648 238*
Tucked beneath the north face of Diffwys, this large 42-acre lake has supplied the Barmouth District with water since it was dammed in 1894. It is thought to be one of only three lakes in Wales to still naturally hold arctic char and also excellent trout. A

legend says that, following a good deed done by a shepherd to the Fairies, they not only put the fish into the lake but also taught him how to catch them – they are known by fishermen to be difficult to catch and according to local belief only one in a hundred has the ability to land them (*The Lakes of Eryri*).

Llyn Caerwch *SH 641 351*
Situated high above the Bronze Age track that runs across the north of the Rhinogydd, this small 5 acre lake is an ideal spot for a

below: Llyn Bodlyn; right: Afon Gamlan

picnic if you are fit as it is a steep climb up to it. On a clear day, there are fantastic views across the whole of the Snowdonia Mountains and the sea towards the Llŷn Peninsular with even a glimpse of Ynys Enlli (Bardsey Island) if you are lucky. '*A large stone with markings that could be interpreted as footprints of man, bird, sheep and ox lies near the track up to the lake. It is called 'Maen ol Troed yr Ych', and tradition claims that a giant threw it down from the lake to its present position*' (*The Lakes of Eryri*). Giants throwing rocks around is a tale told about nearly every large stone found in an unusual position in north Wales!

Afon Gamlan

The source of Afon Gamlan is in the glacial lake of Llyn y Bi, which is tucked beneath Rhinog Fach and Y Llethr. It flows past Cefn Gam Slate Quarry down to Ganllwyd village where it joins the Mawddach. It tumbles over a series of rocky steps and finally ends in a magnificent waterfall – Rhaeadr Ddu just above the village. The falls have been a tourist attraction since Victorian times and the beautiful gorge carved by the river is renowned for the richness of its moss, fern and lichen flora. A canopy of ancient oak woodland encloses the turbulent waters providing a high humidity level that is perfect for these plants – every rock, trunk and branch is covered in a green carpet.

This is the historic parkland of the Dolmelynllyn Estate where the impressive oaks were used for building houses and boats and their bark used in local tanneries. The Plas was once the home of William Madocks, builder of Porthmadog's famous Cob, and amongst those who helped him raise the money was his great friend and poet, Percy Bysshe Shelley – Information: National Trust.

Afon Cwmnantcol

From its source in the tiny Llyn Cwmhosan high up on the rocky slopes of Rhinog Fawr and Rhinog Fach, this beautiful river flows south-west through Bwlch Drws Ardudwy, following an ancient road used by the drovers. The Cwmnantcol flows in majestic meanders, just like a miniature Mississippi, across ancient field systems beneath rocky cliffs littered with manganese mines.

The river passes through the pretty village of Llanbedr on its journey to the sea where it culminates in a wide estuary near Llandanwg. Llandanwg was strategically placed on the best anchorage in north

Wales and Bronze Age roads connect it with the Dee and Severn valleys. Sitting here almost buried by the sand dunes, can be found a Grade II listed church, dedicated to Saint Tanwg. The earliest parts of the church date back to the 13th century making it one of the oldest Christian sites in Britain. It is also the longest continuing place of Christian worship with services still being held here today.

Shirley Toulson writes in *The Drovers' Roads of Wales* – '*Here are memorials to the Roberts family and John Roberts was one of*

Afon Cwmnantcol

the last recorded drovers from these parts; the Roberts family were christened, married and buried in this church'.

The Ingenus Stone, a pillar stone that stands by the altar, is 2.4 metres in length and weighs ¾ of a ton. It is inscribed with the name '*INGENUS*' and is believed to date back to the 5th century. It may have come from the Wicklow Hill in Ireland as the stone is made from rock not found in Meirionnydd. (www.snowdoniaheritage).

Livestock and Other Animals

Welsh Mountain Sheep

On a visit to Dolgellau Farmers' Mart I watched the judging of Welsh Mountain rams and what magnificent beasts they are with their wonderful curled horns! At the auction that followed, the best-in-class rams were fetching thousands of guineas – an old coinage used instead of pounds for the auctioning of top animals (a guinea is worth £1 and 1 shilling – £1 and 5 pence in new money).

According to the Welsh Mountain Sheep Society: '*They are one of the oldest*

left: Llandanwg Church; right: Welsh Mountain sheep

sheep breeds in the world, it is still as important today as any other breed. They are economical, hardy and make excellent mothers. Other advantages are they are inexpensive to purchase, lamb easily and require little additional feed'.

Ty Newydd, a ruin near Pont Scethin, once thought to be a coaching inn, was actually two terraced houses for tenant shepherds of Corsygedol Estate. Tommy O'Mara and William Baddell lived there in the early 1900s and fell out in a big way when one accused the other of sheep stealing. The case went to court at the Dolgellau Assizes but when the meat was examined it was found to be long dead. When the Judge discovered that the shepherd had been feeding his starving family on old carcases found in the hills, he dismissed the case.

The tiny little lambs are so beautiful and to see them jumping around, playing chase and 'king of the castle' on a sunny evening in spring is a delight to behold!

Welsh Black Cattle

The Welsh Black Cattle Society (Cymdeithas Gwartheg Duon Cymreig) state *'They are Wales' only native breed and their story is steeped in history and they are equally at home in craggy uplands or lush lowland pastures. This hardy breed provides high quality meat and milk'*. I have seen massive bulls being led sedately around the judging arena at Dolgellau by young lads looking so proud to have been given this special role.

It is a truly inspiring sight to see these magnificent cattle with the sunlight glistening on their coats on the mountain pastures of Cwm Bychan, Cwm Nantcol and on the slopes above Corsygedol.

The calves are born black, but some of them turn a beautiful dark mahogany colour with black around their eyes before finally changing back to black again at about 9 months. The Welsh Blacks are a long-lived breed and a cow at Gerddi Bluog Farm, named Gerddi Dilys 4, is 23 years old – one of many know to be over 20.

The magnificent head of a black bull looks down from a wall in the main theatre at Ceredigion Museum. It had previously been on display in the butcher's shop of Peter Mathews until it closed. It was then moved to a place of honour over Peter's bed but his wife gave an ultimatum *"Either it goes or I do!"* – so henceforth it was given to the Museum (Information: Stuart Evans – Ceredigion Museum).

Feral Mountain Goats

Although there are few cattle passing through the Rhinogydd today, herds of feral goats can be spotted roaming the mountains. On a previous visit to Cwm Nantcol two large herds melted away on

my approach. At mating time the males get very smelly and this is often the first indication that they are around! According to the Guardian, '*They are shaggy symbols of national independence and a well-loved feature of the landscape of North Wales that have roamed Snowdonia for 10,000 years*'.

A steep gorge that runs down from the Clogau Mine to Bont-ddu has the curious name Uffern y Geifr and this is thought to be because it is so precipitous, moist and slippery, with its sides covered with mosses, that not even a goat could safely traverse its ledges!

Meirionnydd has a new flag! *Three 'dancing' goats and the sun are featured on the striking blue and yellow Meirionnydd flag; it was registered on 2 January 2015 and derived from the seal used by the former Meirionnydd County Council. This, in turn, was based on a description of a banner borne by the men of Meirionnydd at the Battle of Agincourt in 1415.*

(www.britishflags.wordpress.com).

Rhinogydd: Ancient Routes and Old Roads

An Endearing Legacy

With its fantastic array of ancient sites and remnants of mine workings to investigate, old trackways to follow and exquisite nature to see, I feel I have given you plenty of reasons to come and explore this wonderful land but remember it is a unique and fragile environment, so please respect this and abide by the following on your visit:

Take only photographs
Leave only footprints
Kill only time

Acknowledgements

It would be impossible to write a book about the history of Meirionnydd without a great deal of help and advice from many people and organisations. The Meirionnydd Archive Offices and the Gwynedd Archaeological Trust have both been especially helpful regarding information and old maps. Also the Ceredigion Museum in Aberystwyth has found unique artefacts for me.

I have listed below people I would like to thank for all their help regarding research, intriguing stories, carrying equipment and 'hotel' accommodation; also the many welcoming farmers who gave me access to their land.

Ken Bridges
Michael & Paula Burnett
Thomas Crowther
Robert Evans
Dave Davis
Maldwyn Davies
Gill Caves
David Coleman
Jacky Cross
Margaret Dunn
Jessica Evans-Williams
Sue & Elwyn Evans – Gerddi Bluog

Robert Evans – Sylfaen
Richard Fisher
Roy Gamblin
Julian Heath
Lowri Jenkins – St Fagans
Peter Jones
Dave Linton – Welsh Mines Society
Arfon Owen – Cae Goronwy
Dr Rhian Parry
Plas Tan y Bwlch
Vanessa Priestley
Alwyn Ellis – Cefn Clawdd
Alun John Richards
David Roberts – Trefri Fawr
Elaine Roberts
John Roberts
Nesta Roberts
Carole Shearman
Angela & Bill Swann
Merfyn Wyn Tomos
Shirley Toulson
Richard Williams
Not forgetting the assistance of Cati the Dog!

I would like to make a special mention of the following people who have helped turn my stumbling words into something suitable for publishing:

Cath Bartlett, Merfyn Wyn Tomos, Dave Linton and especially Twm Elias and Kate Coldham!

Further Reading / Useful Contacts

Anyone seeking historical information about Wales should contact the following:

Bangor University Library Archive
Ceredigion Museum – Aberystwyth
Gwynedd Archive Offices – Caernarfon and Dolgellau
Gwynedd Archaeological Trust – Bangor
National Library of Wales – Aberystwyth
National Monuments Record of Wales – Aberystwyth
St Fagans – Museum of Welsh Life – Cardiff

Books Used for Reference
Mining

A Gazetteer of the Welsh Slate Industry – Alun John Richards
Echoes of the Gold Rush by the Mawddach – Brian Slyfield
Now You Know: Royalty – Doug Lennox
Metal Mines of North Wales – C J Williams
Merionethshire – T A Morris
The Gold Mines of Meirioneth – G W Hall
Treasurers of the Mawddach – H J Owen

Drovers

Hard Road to London – Idris Evans
Welsh Cattle Drovers – Richard J Colyer
Roads and Trackways of North Wales – Tim Prevett
The Drovers' Roads of Wales – Fay Godwin & Shirley Toulson
The Roads & Trackways of Wales – Richard Moore Colyer
Wales and the Drovers – Philip Gwyn Hughes

General

A Guide to Ancient & Historic Wales – Frances Lynch
A Tale of Two Rivers – Alun John Richards
Atlas Meirionnydd
Circular Walks in Meirionnydd – Dorothy Hamilton
Elizabethan Wales – Geraint Dyfnallt Owen
Gerald of Wales – The Journey Through Wales Translated: Lewis Thorpe
Great Walks North Wales – Frank Duerden
Hanes Trawsfynydd (A History of Trawsfynydd) – Merched y Wawr
Highways & Byways in North Wales – A G Bradley
History of Meirioneth Vol 1/11 – Bowen & Gresham
Life and Tradition in Rural Wales – J Geraint Jenkins
Meini Meirionnydd – Huw Dylan Owen

Merionethshire – Cambridge County Geographies
Nannau – Philip Nanney Williams
Snowdonia from the Air – Peter Crew/Chris Musson
Stage Coaches in Wales – Herbert Williams
The Cambrian Coast – Pwllheli to Harlech – Editor: Ioan Roberts
The Lakes of Eryri – Geraint Roberts
The Mawddach Ardudwy Trail – David Berry
The Snowdonia National Park – W M Condry
Tudor Wales – W S K Thomas
Walks Around the Rhinog – Michael Burnett
Welsh History Book 2 – A J Roderick

About Jean Napier

Born in the East End of London, Jean has lived in the Snowdonia National Park since 1991 and the magnificent variety of scenery within Eryri is the main inspiration for her work. Man's archaeological and industrial influences on the landscape are a recurring theme in her exhibitions, films and books.

Her primary motivation is to promote photography as an artform; using the camera as a creative tool to explore and interpret, not just a means for recording moments in time.

Her work has been widely exhibited in the UK, and in the USA and Australia. She runs photography workshops for people of all ages and abilities throughout the UK including a long-standing series of Landscape Photography Workshops at the Snowdonia National Park's Study Centre at Plas Tan y Bwlch, Maentwrog.

She holds a Masters with Distinction in Fine Art (Photographic & Film Studies) and is an Associate of the Royal Photographic Society.

www.jean-napier.com